I0503667

Procrastination - the Thief of Time

The Procrastinators' Book, Including Strategies and Practical Methods for Getting Rid the Procrastination Habit and Laziness

Sandra Caswell

ISBN: 978-1-7124-9151-5

Table of Content

Introduction

Simple Guide to Solving Complex Problems Related to Procrastination by Developing Self-Discipline to Increase Productivity. To enable you to do more in less time and live a joyful life.

Raise your hand up, if you are in a perfect relationship; enjoy financial stability, in great health and shape. You feel great, live in harmony with family, friends, have an ideal job, or run a booming business.

Put your hand down if there is a lack in one, two, three, or all of these areas of your life. What is stopping you from enjoying most, if not, all of these life's pleasures? Your guess is as good as mine. Procrastination follows you around everywhere in at home, workplace, in the business, marriage relationship and social life.

"Nothing is so fatiguing as the eternal hanging on of an uncompleted task," Professor William James, known as the father of applied psychology, observed.

Putting off tasks influences your physical, psychological, and spiritual well-being. You have a wonderful body and brain capable of creating the situation you desire in life. You blame external forces for your woes and failure to live on the top level of life.

You have read books, listened to motivational speeches on how to stop procrastinating. But until you identify the cause of procrastination, your lifetime ambition remains a pipe dream. So how do you stop procrastinating?

In a nutshell, this book shows you how to challenge procrastination. Chapter one defines procrastination, points out the reasons why you procrastinate and offers techniques on how to distinguish procrastination from idleness.

Chapter two presents tested and trusted methods of discovering signs and symptoms of procrastination. In addition, you will understand the causes and consequences of procrastination.

Chapter three treats you to strategies and practical methods of getting rid of procrastination. This book concludes by inviting you to welcome change as the first step towards a new life of freedom.

Who Should Read this Book?

This book weaves together practical life experience stories and strategies of individuals who confronted procrastination and live to tell their story of determination to works to eliminate procrastination. Think book is your road map to the next level in life.

Chapter 1 - Types and Ways to Counteract Procrastination

Defining Procrastination

One-fifth of the adult population and 50% of students procrastinate, research study outcome reveals. Procrastination can influence physical and psychological stress. A lot has been achieved to explain the causes and consequences of procrastination. Researchers are at work to discover conclusive evidence on the root cause of procrastination.

What is procrastination? How do you differentiate procrastination from idleness? Chapter one answers these two questions, points out five common types of procrastination, examines three reasons why you procrastinate and shows you how to handle such situations.

Procrastination is an acquired habit of putting off tasks you should do now. Reasons different people give to justify this habit vary in degree from one person to the next. Joe's story is an excellent illustration of procrastination in modern living.

Doctors did not give Joe half a chance to live beyond ten days. He was in a coma for two weeks. Joe was treated on and off for malaria prior to this incident.

Jerry, Joe's clinician friend, recommended further medical tests. Joe did not take him up this suggestion until he went down with acute bout of meningitis. Joe woke up from the two-week comma, partially blind, imbalanced and stone-cold deaf. That is a huge price to pay for procrastination.

How long does hospital tests take? One, two, three hours at most. That is a small price to pay to prevent procrastination. How do you distinguish laziness from procrastination?

3 Common Types and 2 Ways to Counteract Procrastination

There are three common types of procrastination: perfectionism obsession, a people pleaser, and possessive fear. Let us isolate these three types of procrastination and clothe them with practical illustrations.

- Perfection Obsession.

Perfectionists are people who strain towards achieving impossible goals. Perfectionist self-worth is measured in terms of success. You have nursed the idea of setting up and running a small online business on the side.

Seven years have passed. You have not taken the first step towards making this dream a reality. It is not for lack of resources. Every detail must be refined and put in place. The business is stuck at the idea stage. How else do you describe this scenario? Perfection obsession has taken over, and procrastination is sitting tight on the driving seat of your life.

You're working to come up with a perfect product or service delivery online.

There is nothing wrong with coming up with the best product/service delivery in the market, perfectionism does not breed procrastination. Balance work and play to allow creativity to flourish. Balancing work is further discussed in chapter three under section seven.

- People Pleaser.

What will people say? You cannot please everyone. You end up throwing away valuable time, energy, and resources trying to impress people. Pleasing people is an excuse to justify procrastination. Get more life out of living. Think about what you want out of life.

You are not an accident of nature. You are different from the rest of humanity, and so is your contribution to society, small or big. You make a difference by looking inside your heart for the hero within. How do you stop the vicious cycle of pleasing people?

Section three discusses the way out under setting achieving goals to prevent procrastination.

- Possessive Fear.

Fear is not in short supply. You fear the unknown. You are afraid of taking time off the business to go on vacation and relax. You are scared of retirement. "What if," the business fails? "What if," this marriage doesn't work out?

These are real fears and concerns about what might go wrong. Fear makes you delay taking action. Fear robs you of valuable energy and dampens your creativity.

Put the energy drained from your body by fear into good use to stop procrastination dead on its track. Turn phobia into productivity with these two ways to counteract putting things off.

Two Ways to Counteract Procrastination.

- Potential Within.

Fingerprints are essential for identification purposes. Your fingerprints are unique and exclusive to you, so is the potential within to accomplish tasks.

"None can duplicate my brush strokes, none can make my chisel marks, none can duplicate my handwriting...." Og Mandino wrote in the book, "The Legend of the Ten Scrolls." So, why let procrastination deny you the opportunity to participate in productivity?

- Productive Participation in the Game of Life.

Life is a chain of activities. From the moment you wake up to the time you retire to bed, you are engaged in one activity after the other. This is great to keep your brain and body in shape for peak performance. Putting off tasks denies is counterproductive.

Joe, in the opening story lead illustration, paid dearly putting off medical checkups. Prevent undesirable outcomes of events by planning g your day to accomplish set tasks. Postponing tasks leads to stress more strain.

You have the potential to influence the outcome of events. Put it into good use. Discover the top three reasons why you procrastinate and how to walk away from them next.

Three Reasons on Why You Procrastinate.

No task is boring, hard or irritating. It is a matter of your interpretation of the task at hand. You postpone carrying out activities based on perception whether the task is dull, hard, and unclear. That is bad news.

The good news is that "anything that has been learned can be unlearned. Anything that has been challenged can be 'relearned,' with a new data to replace the old," Maxwell Maltz wrote in "Psycho-Cybernetics 2000," book.

The research traces this behavior of putting things off back centuries ago.

"Time inconsistency," in Behavioral Psychology research, shows the human brain is more sensitive to immediate incentives than delayed future gratification. The idea of using incentive to replace procrastination is discussed in section three of this book.

Individuals set goals to improve present and future lifestyle. Actions to achieve these goals take place in the present. Delay or postponement influences set goals outcome, now and in the future. Three reasons top the priority list on why you procrastinate and how to walk away from it.

Let's consider two types of tasks vulnerable to procrastination and how to handle them.

Two Types of Tasks Vulnerable to Procrastination.

It is difficult but not impossible to put the finger on specific reasons why you react to one set of activities differently from others.

Procrastination is linked to how you feel about distinct tasks. Emotions are abstract. You cannot reach, and change feelings the way you change clothes. Two types prone to procrastination stand out.

- Difficult Tasks Frighten You.

Difficult tasks are terrifying and discouraging. It is difficult but not impossible to find a way out of this situation. It is easy to put off jobs which frighten you. You get breathing space. But the task is unresolved. That is the challenge.

Resolution: Simplify the Task.

You love to learn to play guitar. You would give anything in the world, including paying top dollar to learn how to play guitar. Enroll and in a course online to learn how to play guitar step-by-step. Manageable bit sizes.

You will be amazed to discover that playing guitar is an organized sense made it simple to tackle unpleasant tasks.

- Unpleasant Tasks Fire up Procrastination.

You love spending time on pleasant tasks. You instead watch television and listen to cool music than take up regular exercise to keep the body in shape. You need more than passing interest to maintain this rhythm.

What is the Challenge? Joe of the opening story was not able to walk without supporting his frail body with a stick. His muscles needed exercise to function in tip-top following one-month long stay in hospital.

He needed to get the body in shape again. The cost of exercise equipment was out of reach. He improvised. Exercising was unpleasant at the beginning.

Any slight body and brain movement were almost unbearable. Joe had a splitting headache, which threatened his resolve. He contemplated giving up several times. However, he kept going. These exercises were his ticket to fully recovery.

Resolution: How much time do you need to go for walks? Grab fresh air, bond with nature, and benefit from a regular dose of exercise during a routine walkabout. Joe threw away the walking stick and began regular activities. He started with five pushups. In a month, he was doing fifty pushups.

Joe also engaged in breathing exercises. He inhaled and slowly exhaled to let the morning into the body and brain. On the tenth count, he held his breathe to a count of 300.

You are into weight lifting but cannot afford gym costs. Use natural stones as weights. In six months, you will notice a huge difference in your body shape.

Pay attention to exercise, whether you want to lose weight or regain body strength like Joe. Learn how to identify signs, symptoms of procrastination, in chapter two, next.

Chapter 2 - Signs, Causes and Consequences of Procrastination

Signs of Procrastination

Your office desk is flowing with paper. The house needs vacuuming. These are signs of procrastination.

Procrastination is a habit you learn. "I shall do that tomorrow," you pronounce without considering the consequences of this simple statement. Putting off stuff is an excuse to justify your inability to make tough choices.

You doubt the potential within. No point in putting off a task you can do today til tomorrow. You have a head start to deal with procrastination, provided you are aware of the signs and symptoms of procrastination. This chapter shows you how to detect the signs and symptoms of procrastination.

Chapter two also reveals causes and consequences of procrastination from individual practical life experience, with good and ready to go measures to take in similar situations. What makes procrastination appealing to the majority of people?

The following seven common signs will draw your attention to identify procrastination and show you how to get out of it.

Six Common Signs of Procrastination

One, Starting Challenge.

You know what you want out of life. That is the easy part. The difficult part is how to achieve your heart desire in life. You have nursed the idea of writing your memoirs for the past seven years.

"I shall take a free online writing course to get the show on the road," you propose, but never get round to it. You use lots of 5-10 or more minutes every day, twiddling your thumbs, idling away.

Solution: "A journey of a thousand miles begins with the first step," A North Korean proverb says. This first step makes the difference. Make a specific date to start writing the memoir. That way, you have a date and dream to fulfill. You are what you think.

Two, utilize Selective Focus.

You cannot carry out all the activities competing for your attention. Pending emails, calls, house chores, physical exercise activities are begging your time and attention. These activities stare you in the eye every day. How urgent are they? That depends on priority.

The important thing is to wrap your head around one activity at a time. You end up spending less time on the activity. This leaves time to spare on for the next item on to-do list.

Solution: Select and focus ding only one task. In photography, it is where the camera lens points, the sharpness of the object in view, that determines the outcome of the print and represents the event long after the party is over.

Selective focusing works well in photography. It will do the same for you in all aspects of life and assist you to shun procrastination.

Three, Running the Race Against Time.

"I don't have time." Yes, you do. You just haven't figured out how to manage the time available on hand. You have acquired tons of carrying forward activities from the past. This is a sign of procrastination having a field day in your life.

Pending activities suck every ounce of energy from your body. This vicious cycle of putting off things started with the first activity. Today, you are drowning in a sea of procrastination with no prospect of a lifeline in view. But, all is not gloom. There is hope for a solution.

Solution: You can wipe procrastination slate clean today. Ask three simple questions to identify and evaluate your past performances.

"Why do I put things off?" Identify different activities you engage in regularly.

"What should I do to stay on top of these activities?" Plan the activities in advance. Schedule a timeline for each activity in the day and stick to it.

"How does it work?" Go through to-do list. Prioritize activities in order of importance.

Four, Look Back, Move Forward.

What comes to mind when you look back in life? Happy and sad moments pop up in the theatre of your imagination. Happy times inspire you. Bad times remind you of wasted opportunities, missed deadlines. "You blew it back then, didn't you," your other half says. Wasted opportunity is the fourth sign of procrastination.

Solution: Give life your best shot in the second chance. Look back and learn from your mistakes to move forward with confidence without procrastination trappings.

Five, There is Room for Improvement.

"Opportunity is everywhere, but it is fleet of foot. Even if you have the vision to recognize it, without a fast decision on your part, it will be gone," Napoleon Hill wrote in "17 Principles of Success," book.

We all have equal opportunities for self-improvement, regardless of child upbringing, culture, or country of origin. Not everyone grabs the opportunity to improve the physical, psychological and spiritual aspects of life.

No one is born an expert in any field. You learn to develop new skills by doing. In the process, you make great progress within short periods with do-it-yourself techniques. You quickly gain fast, effective ways to deal with procrastination.

Solution: Use the clock, and calendar to guide and assist you to gauge performance progress. Students, who put off regular study time, fail exams. Employees get fired from work for missing deadlines. Clients expect the delivery of goods and services on a promise. Do not wait for the eleventh hour. You will be time-barred. Do it now!

Six, Pull of the Past.

You live in the present; think of the future, yet the mind dwells in the past. Your mind is preoccupied with past mistakes that have come back to haunt you.

This is another reason why you put off activities. You cannot undo past blunders. You can correct course them, and so doing kick procrastination out of your system. It is doable.

Solution: Identify the tasks you need to accomplish now. Sort the activities related to these tasks in order of priority. Pick and work on one activity or task to completion. This way, you crowd out procrastination signs. You also need to recognize procrastination symptoms.

Symptoms of Procrastination and Remedy

You lose hair every time you run a comb through the head. Not a significant portion. But the single strands that fly off the head make all the difference with time. This happens all the time. You might have just noticed. But the symptoms have been there all along.

Several facts determine symptoms of procrastination. Five of the most recognized symptoms include fear of change, saving time, disorganization, distractions, and tiredness.

- Fear of Change Freaks You Out.

Fear of not coping with change presents most people with enormous challenge. You are at ease until it descends and stirs your cozy life.

The action of the mother eagle best illustrates this point. All is well with the eaglets until the mother eagle decides, it is time for the broods to learn to fly. She rips the nest and pushes the eaglets out against their will. The eaglets are forced to learn to flap their wings or fall to the ground.

This similar scenario plays in the life of human beings. Most changes are caused by chaos. Financial setback, when the business flops. Grief over the death of loved one, sickness among others, bring change, which freaks you out.

Remedy: In the case of a financial setback in business. Take Stock. Retrace your steps back to where the company began making losses.

Evaluate the situation to make adjustments. This requires making tough decisions. Take up the challenge head-on. Ignoring or putting off these steps is a recipe for disaster.

- Lack of Vision Leads to Hopelessness.

A good vision evaluates the past, examines the present, and expresses the desire for future achievement. Your vision communicates inner desire. Vision is the North Pole reference point in the home, work, and business. A vision is achieved through strategic thinking.

"Strategic thinking...links where you are to where you want to be," Dr. J.C. Maxwell in the book "Thinking for A Change," noted. Strategic thinking begins with set clear standards.

Remedy: Set clear set to create a common ground of understanding in the home, workplace and business, the three areas prone to procrastination.

Two, Clear Set Standards Motivate People to Achieve Goals.

Three, clear set standards define expectations.

Time is Priceless Commodity.

Activities take place within specific time frames. Time contributes to the outcome of activities in the home, workplace and in business. The result of activity is determined by the quality of the hours spent.

Your life runs on time. Spending time in front of the television is good entertainment, but a poor investment of time.

Remedy: You only have 24 hours in a day to spend. No more. No less. Budgeting time on hand is the best solution. Get organized. Save time by scheduling tasks.

Section three-under time management, details the significance of keeping time.

- Feeling Tired and Lost in the Crowd.

You fear taking time off work or business. You have time to catch up with the latest gossip in town, but not to go on vacation to relax to avoid body and brain overload.

It is any wonder you are tired and worn out. You think putting off this or the other activity is the easy way out. You are dead wrong. Procrastination does not remedy the situation.

You end up growing more tired, twiddling your thumbs idling time away than engaging in productive activity.

Remedy: Take these three simple steps to get back, of course. First, describe the task in writing. Second, break down the activities into smaller, manageable sizes. Third, take action.

- Dispose of Distractions.

The world has gone digital. Technology is neutral. This is welcome news and worrying concern. Welcome, because there is no monopoly on available information on the internet.

It is a worrying concern that kids as young as five years old have access to all content, including adult stuff in the comfort of the homes and convenience of the Smartphone.

Technology is the biggest distraction in modern-day living. You would be hard-pressed to manage incoming flux of business calls, and working to a deadline. A recent study shows the phone could rob you 20% work input if it is within reach of the working environment.

You can't have enough of what you don't want. You might not cut off all access to technology if your business life cycle depends on it.

Remedy: Get off social media. Slow down on emailing. Only leave apps you cannot do without on the phone. Back down from technology to avoid burn out. Discover causes and consequences of procrastination, and you are on the way out to a good start in life.

Causes and Consequences of Procrastination

On the one hand, there are skilled procrastinators. On the other hand, mild procrastination is an equally harmful retrogressive habit. The rest fall in the middle of these two extremes.

Whether you have practiced and perfected, or struggling to keep your head above the water level of procrastination. You won't regret dropping procrastination fast.

You remember Joe in the opening lead story. Today, Joe is consigned to live the rest of his life deaf for putting off regular medical checkups. This delay gave meningitis disease time to mature and become acute. He paid dearly for procrastination.

Joe was trained as a sound engineer. His ears were the most significant assets, until they turned into greatest liability. Putting off this one activity caused Joe permanent hearing loss and a lifetime of consequence in the silent world of the deaf. What is the worst-case scenario for postponing your tasks?

Stress in the Family.

Miriam and Matthew were happily married for five years before cracks of conflict showed up in the relationship. Miriam's two kids, Mark ten and Betty seven, she brought into this marriage relationship, did not make the situation easy for the couple.

Mark had difficulty adjusting to the new father figure in his life. Miriam, not using much discretion, took sides with her son Mark. Tension and pressure increased between the two making the situation worse.

"I am stressed," Miriam blurted out one evening when she couldn't take any more simmering rivalry in the house.

"What is stressing you, my dear?" Mathew inquired calmly. But the writing was already on the wall. None of them was willing to back down.

Your stress hormones are triggered by several factors, worry is one of them. You lose sleep over imaginary problems, laugh less, and are irritated by trivial comments.

Miriam eventually walked out on Mathew. She made no effort to patch things with Matthew. She had no time to adjust and cope with stress.

What is stress? Donald Norfolk a British osteopath who has made a significant study on stress, observed that stress comes from two leading causes: "too little change or too much change." In Miriam and Matthew's case, the change might have been both.

Business Bankruptcy.

In another development, Michael hired an individual consultant to assist in improving productivity in the business he purchased from the previous owner. That was spot on. The consultant proposed a change from analog to digital in his report.

This time coincided with the introduction of Compact discs in the market. Analog videotape, mainstay product of the video library business was heading out.

Michael read the report and acknowledged that the wind of digital was gaining momentum, and would soon blow over analog. However, he was reluctant to inject capital into the business.

In less than three years before the business could break even, the business wound up. True to the consultant's prediction, a digital wind of change swept analog business.

The one thread running through the above three causes and Consequences is procrastination. In the case of Miriam and Matthew, stress outcome drove the last nail on the coffin of the relationship.

Michael's business went belly up. You have been down a couple times.

You did not fall to pieces when the business went belly up. You scraped through bitter divorce proceedings. You did not give up during any of these situations. You bounce back to life. You can do it again when procrastination camps on the doorstep of your heart.

Joe learned valuable lessons from the encounter with procrastination. A similar opportunity is available for you. Here is Joe's experience.

Joe Bounced Back from Procrastination. You can as well.

Joe did let procrastination take control of his life. His old life was ancient history. But the future was a virgin land with a great prospect. He embarked on an ambitious self-improvement mission.

Joe evaluated his past life to identify areas that could still be changed.

Second, he emphasized using hidden potential in preparation to take the next big step in life.

Third, Joe visualized the expected outcome in advance to assist him in navigating the rough train on the long road to bounce back to life. Joe's experience is unique and exclusive to him. Bu the principles to overcome procrastination is free and available to you. Here are five super simple methods to overcome procrastination.

Three Super Simple Methods to Overcome Procrastination

- Magnitude of the Task.

You come up to a challenging task and think, "Wow! This is huge. I shall never get done with it." That is the old procrastination playback stalking you. Yes, you will. You have done it before. You can do it now.

You carry out different tasks daily with success. You don't have to do them all at once. Break the activities down into small parts. This makes the task less intimidating. Performing a series of activities provides variety and eases the pressure of monotony.

Practical Way Out: Farm work is broken down into smaller activities. First, you clear the field. Second, prepare the soil. Third, you plant or transplant seedlings from the seedbed. Fourth, weeding and tending to plants.

You are recovering from sickness. Make your way through hard situations one step at a time. You carry on one moment, and then another and the day is over. You rest overnight a

- Mix and Match Activities to Create Variety.

You are intelligent and creative. You think, plan and act upon challenging activities with great success. Mix and match different activities to create variety and beat boredom in studies.

Practical Way Out: How much time do you need for research, class or regular lecture assignments? Set a specific time for each of these academic study activities. Determine which activities can be lumped together. For example, while researching online, craft the outline of the essay paper as the computer loads content on the screen.

Switching between these two activities does not require a great deal of concentration as studies for an exam. Download online content to save time and read through it at a different time.

- Overwhelmed, Motivation is Running Low.

Your online entrepreneurship life cycle depends on the delivery of product/service. You have won a tender to supply a consignment of goods. The deal is lucrative. This is what you have been waiting for to take the business to the next level.

This is exciting. It is also intimidating. You do not have all the stuff to pull this deal off the ground. No business is 100% equipped to handle a large order of goods required urgently.

Practical Way Out: Solicit assistance from a trusted friend. You could need expert advice to improve productivity, speed up the process, and build confidence to deliver on a promise.

Joe sought David's assistance to establish an online freelance writing business. Joe could no longer use his sound engineer training having lost hearing. He had to change careers. Freelance writing was the next best opportunity.

Chapter 3 - Strategies and Practical Methods of Getting Rid of Procrastination

This chapter on strategies and practical methods of getting rid of procrastination walks you through the process of kicking procrastination out of the way.

You will learn the significance of lifting off the lid of limitation. Reflect on rewards. Set achievable goals. Acknowledge the nature of internal communication. How to schedule tasks. Balance work and play. Plan and make time for meditation to boost your energy level.

Let's get started on these strategies and practical methods.

Section 1- Rule of three Revolves around Necessity, Deliberation, and Action

You have a vision of the kind of family life, work, or business which suits your taste and resonates with your core values. Razor-sharp vision determines the purpose. Purpose defines actions.

Let's dive in and discover how the rule of three works in relation to the strategies and practical methods of getting rid of procrastination this book advocates in this chapter.

- Need Identity.

The reason you struggle with procrastination has nothing to do with distractions from outside. It has everything to do with poor self-image frown within. Henry Dyke, declared that, "Some people are so afraid to die that they never begin to live."

In the context of this book, you are afraid to drop procrastination that success is remote and removed. You alone hold power to push procrastination out of your life and attract prosperity.

- Reflection on Life.

You miss dancing to the rhythm of the music in the home, workplace owing to lack of concentration. Channel your interest, attention, and efforts on the single task ahead to accomplish the task at hand.

Create tailor-made practice. How effective is your day-to-day schedule? Use this schedule to gauge performance to determine practice effectiveness. The score on a scale of 1-10 mirrors your commitment to productivity.

Revise your goals and activities periodically to prevent procrastination pitfalls. This is the secret behind creating tailor-made practice.

- Action-Packed Activities.

"Action speaks louder than words," is not just another overused, tired cliché. This time tested truth pays back big time. Work on ways to overcome procrastination today. Not tomorrow. Not when your life is in a crisis. Do it now!

Section 2 - Lift the Lid of Limitation to Overcome Procrastination

The spider web is an artistic masterpiece work to achieve by this small insect. Each strand is weaved onto the web. This repetitive work of spinning strands, joining each strand to the body takes time and patience.

Difficult as it sounds to construct the spider web, the finished product is done with finesse. The small tasks determine the overall outcome. Nature supplies the spider with material and necessary skills to accomplish this task.

You have superior natural skills and knowledge at your disposal to undertake any task, including getting rid of procrastination.

"Great people do things before they're ready... doing what you're afraid of, getting out of your comfort zone, taking risks like that -- that's what life is," Amy Poehler confirmed.

- Engage in Tasks on Short Period of time.

You need around five minutes to brush your teeth in the morning. You spend half-hour on breakfast, ten minutes to dress up, between forty-five minutes to one hour on the road to the office. This is a similar pattern with a slight variation of activities.

The day is made up of a series of small tasks. You don't rub your hands together and say, "Now, let's see. How much time can I spare on this and that small tasks? You simply do one after another. You perform many small tasks at the close of a day without fussing over the lid of limitation.

- Establish Peak Performing Hours.

Most people achieve a lot more work in the early part of the day. Take advantage of this time of day to handle difficult tasks. Your source of headache is business accounts. There is little money to hire an expert.

Get on with it. A business account is not rocket science. Learn if you must. Make time for this activity; you are more resourceful.

- Increase Perform through Self-confidence.

"When a baby is learning to walk, he/she falls many times...He/she may cry for a while... but he/she always gets back up and tries again and again," Joyce Meyer wrote in a column on "Living Well," titled "Stay Positive, Refuse to Give Up."

A baby believes in its self. Belief in yourself is not exclusive to kids. Adults embark on numerous tasks daily based on belief in self. Belief in self is based on facts. It's more accurate.

Turn away from the trap of distrusting yourself by recalling to memory the exceptional moments you were at your best.

Section 3 - Incentive System

Think of the thrill you feel at the end of the successful completion of a task. The author's name on the cover of the book, for example, brings the best out of the writer.

The paycheck is great. But the privilege of standing shoulder to shoulder with renowned authors in the industry boosts your personality and carries the day. Reflection on the reward gives you the drive to take on seemingly impossible challenges.

Take a break from the usual environment. Plan to finish the book manuscript, report, or creation of a new product line for the business in a different holiday location. The new place offers a great deal for relaxation.

Get inspired by sightseeing, trying out different cuisines, meeting new people, and taking short walks around the place. These are invaluable rewards. You leave the place re-reenergized, writing battery recharged in addition to finishing writing the manuscript in record time.

Section 4 - Separation of Responsibility and the Ability to Say - No!

Watching TV, surfing the net chew valuable time to exercise tired muscles, engage in weight loss activities. You have always wanted to become a painter. Take up lessons to improve on the skill.

Watching television is a one-way conversation. Your mind is running but in neutral. If you are to learn to develop the art of communication, turn off the TV. Conversation is talking and listening. You don't get the opportunity of talking back to the characters on television.

If you are going to think, read, and write, then you must disengage from watching television. Learn to separate responsibilities from pleasure to manage your time wisely. The reason you do not have enough time is that everything is lumped together. You run the risk of procrastination.

Procrastination has put a dent in your life. You are angry, miserable. You live from hand to mouth. It is not late. You can reverse the trend. Take procrastination on by the horn.

- Verify your values.

"Values" are accepted standards in life. The two words put together to give meaning to this word and provide conventional rules governing life. Think of the importance of five fingers to your body.

Values determine beliefs. Beliefs define expectations. Expectation drive outcome in life. You can do this with proper time management.

"God broke the years to hours and days." This first line in the poem by George Klingle, "Hour by Hour," summarizes the importance of breaking down tasks into manageable sizes.

- Lack of Motivation.

You cannot impress everyone, no matter how good your product or service delivery. This does not mean the product or service is substandard. Feedback from customers should not discourage you from losing motivation. Motivation is a combination of two words "Motive" and Action. Simply stated, motivation is a motive in action.

You imagine a better life. But inadequacy in health, finance, family, or other aspects of life does not make it easy to live a fruitful and fulfilled life. You are overwhelmed. Your body range of power is at a record low. You lack the motivation to stay on course.

If you were to write every line of the book to perfection, from start to finish, the book would take longer to finish. Write a page, two-three when creativity is high, then proofread and correct.

This method promises a fast turnaround. Brooding over every single sentence to make it perfect does the reverse. It slows you down. You lose motivation. This leads to procrastination and eventual lack of motivation.

- Enjoy What You Love Doing.

You're working too hard: you need to relax. Urban dwellers and affluent societies turn into hobbyists and craft persons to maintain doing what they do. Think of it as another form of incentive discussed in section three above.

Painting, jewelry making, weaving, gardening, modeling, photography, ceramics, writing are common vocations. The main reason is to enjoy doing what they love with a sidekick activity.

Routine is boring regardless of how much you love the activity. A side hustle spices up the routine. Refresh your memory with the advantages of breaking away from routine activities discussed in section three above.

Section 5 - Prioritization Based on Personal Goals

A housewife desires to make things work well around the house. She values her family. She is in the middle, restricted by family obligations and house chores.

She is under pressure of personal growth, family, business, health, finance, fitness, and spirituality. Restrictions upon her life create emotional tension, which usurps strength leaving her exhausted. This scenario is not exclusive to housewives. The effect of pressure is felt at the place of work, business, and society. Society expectation is driving many fine individuals down the path of destruction.

How do you handle these situations without carving under pressure or becoming a victim of procrastination? Set achievable personal goals.

- Set Achievable Personal Goals.

You don't pack your bags and leave home without knowing where you are going, how to get there or why you are making the journey in the first place. In your dreams, you do. In real life, you set goals.

"A goal is a statement of commitment to carry out specific tasks in a given period of time." Writing this book generated three questions.

1. What do you want to do? Write a book on Procrastination?

This question seeks to express heart desire - Purpose.

2. How long will this it take to write this book?

This is the process question intended to reveal a time frame.

3. Why write this book?

This is the outcome question - Product.

What kind of personal, professional, relationship, financial status, health, family, or spiritual goals do you wish to achieve in life? If you have not taken life membership in the spectators club with the majority, achieving an ideal future life is far-fetched and unattainable.

You have tried several times, but you were held hostage by procrastination. Your attention is diverted, and the focus shifted from the primary goal. You were unable to marshal the courage to become the person you desire in life.

Not all is lost. Do it with a difference this time round to prevent procrastination from running and ruining your expectations. Take these three simple steps to get what you want in life.

Three Steps in Setting Achievable Goals

- Sort Out Your Life.

You have accumulated the good the bad and ugly in the past. These are items, thoughts, and anything else in your keeping. You have not had time to go through any of this stuff.

All of them have been chucked together for self keeping. You go through a laborious painful process to pick out an item you need. This procedure scares the living daylight in your life.

Your life is in a rut. It is time for a change. It is not difficult to go through files, letters, household items, and clothes to sort out what you don't. It is also easy to dispose of these items.

For example, rummage through the wardrobe and take out clothes you have not used in the past six months or one year. You can sell or give them out to charity organizations.

Heck, sorting out negative from positive thoughts is a lot more complicated than pinching old clothes from the wardrobe to give away. You have put this exercise off far too long, and it is affecting your progress in life.

No more procrastination. Get it done today and show procrastination the door out of your life.

Sorting out your life is the first step to avoid chasing the wind. Besides, you create more room for positive thoughts.

Negative thoughts and old beliefs hang on to you like the shadow. Shaking negative thoughts around without replacing them with positive thoughts is a temporary measure. The moment the sensation fades out. Boom! Negative thoughts are back on course, and procrastination swing into action.

The best solution and only solution is to replace defeating negative thoughts with positive productive.

- Tap into Hidden Talents.

"You can heat a kettle of water to boiling point in ten

minutes without using electricity...wood or gas fuel..," Keith and Irene observe in the Australian Self-Sufficiency Handbook, 'A Survival Guide for the 21st Century."

This principle also works in conserving energy as well as in self-improvement. You achieve set goals by focusing attention on tasks related to the specific purpose. Setting achievable goals requires breaking down goals into short, medium and long-term.

- Separate Short, Medium, and Long-term Goals.

Separation of short, medium, and long term goal(s) allow you to enjoy the victory of goal achievement. Short-term goals relate to activities that require action now.

Medium goals bridge the gap between short and long-term goals. Learning a new skill falls under medium-goals. You are working 9-5 day job. You wish to start and run a small business on the sides to subsidize your income. The new skill comes handy. It is easy on the pocket and time. Take evening classes or online courses comfortably.

Long-term goals range from two years and above. You might classify building a house under a long-term goal. This is a project that requires substantial capital investment. It also takes time.

- Select Your Goals Wisely.

Select goals in order of importance. Assign tentative completion dates. Be flexible to adjust time to suit your plan. Check out the following seven areas that are open to personal goals.

- Seven Areas of Goal Setting.

1. Personal Growth Goals - Arts, Music, Writing...
2. Health & Fitness Goals - Exercise, Nutrition, Weight.
3. Family & Relationship Goals – Family, Friendship & Fun
4. Finance Goals - Investments, Debts, & Charity.
5. Work/Career Goals - Jobs, Skills, and Entrepreneurship.
6. Education & Training Goals - College & Graduate

School Technical Skills.

7. Spiritual / Ethical.

Section 6 - Fighting Internal Criticism

Listen to the inner voice to identify the nature of internal communication. Your inner voice will warn and prompt you to take action. The inner voice is the mechanic for the body system. The body needs rest from time to time. The alert body alarm system sends the message to all parts of the body. You yawn. The eyes get heavy. It is time for a snooze.

You know that the body needs nourishment. You are famished. The stomach is growling. Your body recoils in pain during sickness. Sweating, shivering are symptoms you might be coming down with a headache.

"Take me to the doctor," the inner voice stirs you up. Ignore it at your own peril.

The inner voice guides you in decision making. There is a war going on between the two personalities, the conscious and the sub-conscious.

You don't know what happens to your shadow when you go to sleep. Just as well. Your shadow goes with you everywhere, and to sleep.

Human shadow is the sub-conscious personality. Although the sub-conscious is passive, it's part of the verbal and non-verbal communication which is the foundation of internal dialogue.

Internal communication influences the outcome of thoughts. This is the backbone of human reasoning, reviews, and reaction. All these three activities take part in the brain and are manifested through the body. Inner conflict occurs between conscious and sub-conscious personalities - minds.

Internal communication is marred by conflict.

"Conflict," is the ...fundamental element of friction...," Janet Barroway said. Individual inner conflict is the source of energy that drives the body to take action. The body is all systems go when your life is in danger. These two are the building blocks of your character.

Section 7 – Striking the Balance Between Work and Personal life

You spend precious time, energy, and resources on things you don't, instead of things you want. Your energy levels high or low vary according to what you are doing and thinking.

Life is sprinkled with one change after another. Change is the cause behind fear of the unknown. Chapter four discusses the process of change in detail and how to manage it. It is important to focus attention on the task at hand. Make that move with these three steps.

Three Steps to Eliminate Pressure.

- Fear of Change.

Change takes place within an environment. In most cases, human beings change is the outcome of chaos. The challenge is to make the most out of bad fear situations.

Fear of change comes from failure and pain. The pain of losing a grip on power is associated with the fluctuation of human emotions. Change is inevitable for the growth and prosperity of the individual and institutions in society. Learn lessons from change.

- Figure Out Your Resourcefulness.

You are capable of making quick and reasonable decisions to deal with other people. You walk, talk, and work long hours, with a high degree of success. You have acquired the ability to carry out complex tasks reasonably well.

Nothing or no one can take these life patterns away from you. These hidden talents kept in the reservoir in your mind. Use them to improve your life.

- Take the Plunge.

Dive into your brain data bank. Pick one talent. Develop it to enrich your life now. You miss golden opportunity to give your life make-over if you put off the activity.

The only prescription drug for pressure is "prioritization"

discussed in section 5 under prioritization based on personal goals. Whiz back there in case you need to refresh your memory with the facts on priority amidst pressure.

Section 8 - Actions that can be completed in 5 minutes - Do-It-Now!

How much work can you accomplish in five minutes? Five minutes is all you need to seal a business deal. In radio broadcasting, five minutes means hooking or losing the audience. Converting five minute talk time into achievement is a significant investment.

High school, college, and university students put off regular study time to hang out with friends. Candidate student beds are deserted near the end of the term, semester. The pressure to excel in exams is at its peak. It is do or die.

Doherty partied hard most nights and weekends. She hardly spent time in the library except when the exams were around the corner. Yet she maintained an "A" mean score throughout her undergraduate study period.

How did she manage to cope with social life and studies? She had a photographic mind. It served her well. You are not Doherty. You don't have a photographic memory. Budget your time and avoid stress. Carry out this exercise at the beginning of the academic term or semester. Here is how it works.

Grab a pen and paper, a laptop computer, or a Smartphone. Sit and write the steps you need to take to excel in studies. Map and block out the timetable with activities daily, week and month.

You won't regret taking these steps.

Section 9 - Making a Realistic to-do list for Every Day

Factors that influence realistic, active schedule include, but not limited to, allowing room for spillover, avoiding cramming large blocks of tasks in a small timeframe. Seven tips will take a realistic, effective balanced schedule fast.

- Focus Full Attention on the Task at Hand.

In a Pone High School physics experiment, the teacher-directed the sun's rays on a single spot on the paper using a magnifying glass. The paper began smoldering in seconds and burst into a flame in less than a minute.

A similar principle can be used to bore a hole through steel by concentrating the sun's rays on one spot. Concentration increases competence. Competence cultivates capability, and capability yields the desired outcome.

Focusing full attention on the task at hand takes away the boredom.

- Slot in Reasonable Accomplishment Time Inside the Schedule.

Identify how much time you require for different activities on a given project. Throw in time allowance, depending on the size of the project.

Individual activities and tasks are unique. Your case is no exception. Determine reasonable, suitable achievement time for the project at hand.

- Discover the Secret Behind Concentration.

There are different activities taking place all around. These activities also compete for your attention. You cannot shut them up. But you can ignore them by concentrating on the task in front of you. Remember, "In a broken nest, there are no whole eggs," the ancient proverb says.

Learn to concentrate. Start with five minutes and build up concentration with time. This is what meditation is all about. Try it out.

- Monitor Your Schedule Progress.

Check your schedule progress from time to time. Monitoring reveals what has been accomplished as well as unaccomplished items in the project. When concentration wanes, take a break.

In television programming, commercial breaks are the parting shots between programs. Commercial break provides the viewer with a good time to run off to the bathroom, or raid the fridge to get a drink.

This is similar to taking short breaks in the project. Stand up. Walk around and stretch. You also need variety in the project to maintain interest. Carry out a different activity in the project, mentioned in the next paragraph down the line.

- Schedule Different Tasks Off Mainstream Project Activities.

Peak performing hours vary in degrees from one person to the next. This is the time you are at your best. Energy is oozing out. You are resourceful. Get more work during this time. Use extra hours off mainstream project activities to answer emails, research, and writing.

Early morning or late at night when family members are out of the way is suitable. Be sure to blend work and play.

- Blend Work and Play.

Balancing the work schedule is significant. Tasks come and go. Life continues. All work without recreation is tedious. You do well to factor time of relaxation into the project schedule.

Grab this opportunity to bond with friends. Get a good laugh. Fun time revitalizes the body and brain. The body is re-energized and good to go on working after a good swim, game of golf, or from family members bicycle ride in the local community.

Section 10 - Long-term Strategic Action Planning

Big Picture Thinking is the ability to visualize the outcome of planned events in advance. In drama writing, you envision characters acting out their parts in the storyline plot.

In drama, scenes in the plot are the building blocks of the strategic action plan. Architects provide a complete building plan. However, the actual building work is done in stages. Digging the foundation precedes other building construction activities on site. The walls are erected once the slab is in place.

Different small and big activities take place in the process of finishing the building. These exercises take time to match accurately to the plan.

A similar long-term strategic action planning principle

applies to other real-life situations, provided you know what you need. Why you need it and how to get it.

Section 11- Nurturing Willpower - A Scientific Approach

Human body renewal is a natural process. The body you showed up in on this planet has gone through a lot of transformation. There is hardly a trace of the original molecules in the present body. You don't notice these changes. But this transformation process continues all the time.

Sleep is the human body recycling therapy procedure. The body system goes to work to repair and replace tired tissues when you are dead asleep. You are as good as new the next day.

Unlike the body, the human brain never takes a break, never goes to sleep during the day and night. The human brain is the only broadcasting station that never goes off the air.

That is the reason behind the scientific approach to beat procrastination. The experimental approach involves four options, namely: the benefits of rewards resulting from taking action, the actual action process, future action plan, and preparation of the ground to achieve goals linked procrastination.

These four options are discussed throughout this book with particular emphasis on strategies and practical methods of getting rid of procrastination.

"With peace in his soul, a man can face the most terrifying experiences. But without peace in his soul, he cannot manage even a simple a task as writing a letter," J.A Hatfield the English psychiatrist wrote in the old book "Psychology and Morals."

Procrastination disrupts the unity of the mind, causes stress and the result, and many other undesirable conditions that lead to human misery.

Section 12 - Meditations to Improve Life Energy

You spend precious energy on things you could do without instead of things you need. Your energy levels vary depending on different odd jobs.

You are capable of attracting what you need in life, as long as it echoes similar sentiments of your core values. If the mind is preoccupied with negative thoughts of failure and regrets, the result is a low disempowering energy level.

Thinking of insufficiency drains energy level fast, leaving the body weak and the mind uncreative.

Think of the moments your heart is on fire to complete a task. Your body energy system booster goes to work. It does not matter that you have been outselling insurance policy, and no one has bought any for the day. Get out there the next day, determined to sell a couple policies.

Keep your mind alert and creative. You make significant progress in selling insurance policies and edge procrastination out of your system.

The opposite happens with a low energy level. Your energy goes to waste. Thinking you don't want to live the impoverished lifestyle the rest of your life is a killjoy statement. The high energy level will convert dreams into reality.

Chapter 4 - Summary

Treating any disease without proper diagnosis is similar to attempting overcoming procrastination without identifying its signs and symptoms.

You know what procrastination is - acquired habit to put off tasks. You are also aware of different types of procrastination, "why," you procrastinate and how to distinguish procrastination from idleness discussed in chapter one.

In chapter two, you discovered signs, symptoms of procrastination. In addition, you learned about the causes and consequences of procrastination.

You were treated to the main course of the book in chapter three on strategies and practical methods of getting rid of procrastination.

Take Away Parting Shot

"The mere fact of knowing what hurts has a curative value," Dr. Hans, world-famous expert on stress, says. Most people prefer the accustomed comfort zone in life. It does not matter what your life is unsatisfactory. You are in denial. That does not bother you. Facing facts to deal with procrastination makes you uncomfortable, and breeds fear.

But there comes a time when, "Every young butterfly struggles for hours to break free from its cocoon. ...if you were to try to help it, it would die. The fight to get out is what develops the strength in its wings ...to fly." That time for now and here. This anonymous quote speaks volumes about the significance of coping with change.

In this final chapter on this book draws your attention to three step-by-step strategy to get rid of procrastination once for all time. The process starts with you.

- Face Your Fears.

Life is cozy in the comfort zone. Change disrupts normal life functions, you think. That is so because you have not stepped out of your comfort zone. Fear is holding you back from taking the next big step in life. That is the real reason why you procrastinate.

Whether you are ready for change or not, change is ready for you.

Strategy: You are thinking of setting up and running a small online business as a side hustle. Share your vision with a friend who is in a similar kind of business. You get free advice and guidance to assist you in taking the next step on the ladder of success.

Bounce business ideas off your friends in confidence. This might be the ticket you need to enter a life of freedom by choice from procrastination.

- Communication is the foundation of all Relationships.

Communication in the home takes place between a husband and wife, parents and children, and between the family and a higher power, many refer to as God.

All these three areas of communication are vital to real happiness in the home office and business. Failure to communicate with one another is the root cause of troubled marriages. Couples in combat risk disconnect by procrastinating to keep the house in order.

Strategy: Discuss and deal with issues of misunderstanding as they come up. In that way, you keep the line of communication free. A small misunderstanding drives a wedge between couples and might blow out of proportion if not resolved.

- Expectation and Preparation for the Next Big Step.

Life is Unpredictable. Maintaining calm in the home, workplace or in business is challenging.

Strategy: Anticipate and prepare for eventualities, stress included. How do you manage this feat? Take these three simple step-by-step strategies to prevent shortcomings in life.

Most people are cagey about new stuff. You put off important things that you can do in five minutes, then turn around and blow away hours on social media, catching up with the latest news, gossip, and unproductive task time.

You catch up with email correspondence when you are supposed to do office work that pays the bills is not a wise career move.

Why postpone tasks that would make your life productive in five minutes? You have reprimanded yourself umpteenth time to plan, act and follow through with tasks many times.

The power bill came in two weeks ago. You put it aside. Five minutes is all you need to pay the power bill through electronic money transfer. Putting off paying electricity attracts a fine. You also risk a delay in reconnection. This could lead to loss of revenue if your work depends on power.

In business, marketing is the bloodline to match the competition and increase productivity. But you let procrastination spoil all the fun and pleasure in life.

Conclusion

One important lesson we can learn from procrastination is the opportunity to rewire your brain. "Change your thinking and your life also changes," J.C. Maxwell wrote in the book "Thinking for A Change." Put the methods outlined in this book into practice to dump procrastination fast.

You don't need a mentor, life coach, or counselor to know that your life is in a rut. It is comforting to know that ditching procrastination is do-it-yourself.

"Yesterday is already a dream, and tomorrow is only a vision. But today well lived makes yesterday a dream of happiness and every tomorrow a vision of hope." This anonymous quote portrays three stages of life, the past, present, and future, open to improvement.

Afterthought

This is a practical guide book to eliminate procrastination. Think of this book as your road map to the next level in life. The book is written from practical life experience about those who encountered and identified procrastination as a habit for putting off important tasks.

This book weaves together practical life experience stories and strategies of individuals who confronted procrastination and live to tell their stories of struggle and sweet success in the end.